Karl Katz Lydén
Poems and Parables
on the Political Utility of Art

Published by

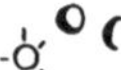

BOM
DIA
BOA
TARDE
BOA
NOITE

Rosa-Luxemburg-Strasse 17
10178 Berlin
Germany
www.bomdiabooks.de

ISBN 978-3-96436-052-6

Book production and layout:
Robin Watkins
Printing and binding:
Zwaan Lenoir

The author would like to thank Jen Hayashida, Martin Högström, Gabriel Itkes-Sznap, Rebecka Katz Thor, Jonas Hassen Khemiri, Lina Rydén Reynols, Robin Watkins, Kim West.

The Deutsche Nationalbibliothek lists this publication in the Deutsche Nationalbibliografie; detailed bibliographic data are available on the Internet at http://dnb.dnb.de.

Printed in the EU

Poems and Parables on the Political Utility of Art

Karl Katz Lydén

Ante Scriptum 5

1. Commodification 19
2. From what marvelous point 33
3. The Barricade 49

Post Scriptum 75
Notes 86

Gorilla on the loose
Close down the zoos

Gorilla on the loose
at the London Zoo

Mid-October drizzle,
armed police response

Helicopters, visitors
scattered 'cross the well-kept lawns

do you really know what to do
when fear (and joy!) comes up the grass
that terrifying moment
when gorilla jumps at glass

This barricade
these shoes

soil
surly news

some songs are written
others are sung

blood
exchange
dust

like snow
falling onto
the bell that rung

this is my song
What happened at Penuel
will happen here as well

In one of today's
undaunted incarnations
of Walter Benjamin and Bertolt Brecht's unborn
journal
Krisis und Kritik
I read

That the modern separation of art and life
is so thorough
that art

remains separated
from *social reality*
as if behind a transparent and impermeable wall

it doesn't matter
whether you put

sculptures in the factory
paintings in the office

whether they are
expressions of beauty or repulsion
works of realism or fantastic representation

not even the Dadaists
dragging toilets and rusty iron bars
into the gallery
managed to escape
domestication

It is,
we learn,
a structural outcome
of the primary
separation, *Abspaltung*, or diremption
of the economic sphere

"The glass prison of modern art consists in this structural
Abspaltung of the aesthetic"

Art is relegated to a ghostlike existence
parallel to the concrete logic of real relations
just like
the social relations of products
lead a separate existence becoming a purpose in itself
in the abstract form of
Money

In the same
dream publication
Another laments art's loss of reality
occurring
just like
narcissism
and commodity fetishism

The second critic invokes
The famous theory of the spectacle
and concludes

Never have there been such long lines
of people waiting outside the exhibitions
And yet,
art suffers from a complete lack of meaning for collective life.

So if someone like Adorno
characterized the products of the culture industry
as incapable of anything but pacification and indoctrination
but salvaged works of high art
as capable of producing a certain negation,
now this position, too, is subsumed.

Art is submerged
like a sunken oboe.

It is not so different from
the art historians' misgivings
about the 1960s neo-avant-garde
or the more recent remarks
on the expansion of the art market
Indeed,
the recurring nature
of this assessment
is one of its main characteristics

It is all summed up
in a recent issue
of an anarchist journal
founded in the 19th century
its thematic section entitled
Art as Fenced-in Area:

either
art amounts to a deceitful production of unreality

or
with time, all attempts to burn holes in the ideological web
merely result in artifacts for the property-owning classes

The critic from Nürnberg is clear:

> All attempts to help art break out of
> its glass prison have failed.

I sit on the balcony
trees and train tracks
fields and phone masts

Only a few leaves left

I sit here and listen
Furrows and filling stations
remote singing
of hairlike railways and bridges

Against the zookeepers
and visitors
convinced of the impermeability
of glass walls

I have three humble objections

First, the question of commodification

1

At the Marah Land Zoo
A photograph of two zebras
(grazing behind a fence)
on the back a news telegram

GAZA (Reuters) – Two white donkeys dyed with black stripes delighted Palestinian kids at a small Gaza zoo on Thursday who had never seen a zebra in the flesh.

Nidal Barghouthi, whose father owns the Marah Land Zoo, said the two female donkeys were striped using masking tape and women's hair dye, applied with a paintbrush.

"The first time we used paint but it didn't look good," he said. "The children don't know so they call them zebras and they are happy to see something new."

The figure of the donkey
appears with some regularity
in the fables of Aesop

The strikingly ugly slave
from Samos who, according to Herodotus,
was freed due to his wits

The figure of labor
The figure of the donkey

A merchant's ass carried bags of sea salt up the mountain. One day it slipped, and fell into a stream. As some of the salt dissolved and the bags got lighter, the ass gaily carried the rest home. The next day, carrying the same amount of salt, the ass, to lighten its burden, fell into the water on purpose. Angered, the merchant returned to the shore, and packed two baskets of sponges. When the ass reached the stream uphill and again performed its trick, the sponges became swollen with water and the weight doubled, making for a heavy walk home.

The fate of the merchant's ass
is not so bad
compared to its kind
in other Aesopian fables

Death by lion
Death by heavy load
Death by drowning

it is more the perpetual defeat
I suppose

being stupid

If ever so slightly cunning,
or, at times, even intelligent

still always
losing

This seems to be the case
at the Marah Land Zoo
the poor asses think they graze
outwitted here too

Unknowingly put on duty
Ridiculed in masquerade
ignorant of the conditions
of surplus extraction
under blockade.

On the other hand
Who gets the last braying laugh?
who has better reasons
to distrust notions of immaterial labor
than an ass?

Starchy
musky and sweet
dry grass
chewed down
to dust

A field day
Make hay

The joyous effect of The Donkey Zebra
is, to some extent, simply
seeing two things at once

the familiar pleasure
of recognizing
a number of
contradictions
embodied in the same figure:

Two species
one animal,

The beastly grazing
and the fabular illusion.

The coat
and the disguise.

The forced labor
and the
no labor

The demonstration of impossibility
and possibility
of *hippo tigris*
in Gaza

So,
there you have it.

For the sake of zookeepers
and visitors
For whom also fables
are impermeable
we shall try to be as clear as possible:

An artwork cannot be taken as any other commodity.

Because art, first of all,
however much it may be an object of consumption
and speculation within capitalism,
does not come about
abiding by the capitalist mode of production.
It does not follow the general formula
of money turned into production of commodities
turned into more money than at the outset
And the reason for that,
quite simply,
is that art does not principally consist
of somebody else's labor,
that which may be called abstract labor, the central commodity
in the production of all other commodities and
the creation of surplus value

It consists of something else entirely.

Consequently, one cannot say
that art leads a ghostlike existence
just like
commodities or money
the former circulating precisely due to
its objective basis in abstract labor
which determines the surplus value
to be realized in the latter

If one takes sponges for salt, one might drown

Second,
in terms I have already established

because artworks can be donkeys.

Finally,
to the extent
that an artwork might actually be a commodity;
(in the simple sense of having an exchange value)

Nowhere does Marx state
that exchange value effaces use value.

It is therefore unclear
why the use value of art
– however evasive –
would be effaced by its circulation
as a tradable good
or, for that matter
its dwelling in a sphere behind glass

We could spell it out with an example
it is the angel of history

For what should be said about *Angelus Novus*?
Paul Klee's monoprint was bought
as a commodity
by Walter Benjamin in 1921

Nineteen years later, it served
as the motif for his ninth
thesis on the Philosophy of History

making its way back

propelled by a storm from paradise
into the antechamber of critical thought

2

From what marvelous point
does this theoretical discourse deliver its judgment on art?

How does it
grasp and reveal, yet evade
the totality
in which art
is caught perpetuating
what it believes to be questioning

It is a simple, perhaps banal question
treading the line of the liar's paradox

(– Everything is a lie.
– Is that true?
– Yes)

Let us follow it to its very conclusion.
Or, at least, try to pose it properly.

How does theoretical discourse
offer the immaculate position
from which it may
dismiss and repudiate
any radical, transformative political utility of art?

How is it capable of the operation
that extends effortlessly to its audience and critically explicates
that art cannot extend anything to anybody,
still less exercise any critical function?

Consider:

α The divide, by which
academically sustained critical theory
is separated from everyday life
– quite like art is said to be separate from *social reality*

β The commodification
of the university itself,
as well as of the circulation of books,
talks and papers
pushed in blurbs and abstracts
by various
surplus-gathering intermediators

Yet unfazed
struck but untouched
by the same phenomena
that paralyzes art,
Theoretical work
conceives of itself
as a message unbound by its media

As if the purity of discourse
would reside in its status
as pure thought

But then
what is thought?

Is it simply this “me or reification”
the my way or the highway
of critical theory?

The idea
transmitted in a kind of pure writing?

(As if we do not sense
the smell of rain hitting stone
the smell of rain hitting asphalt
the smell of rain hitting soil
In the unresolved tension
between a rational, a speculative, and a critical
mode of production)

It does seem unwise to
monopolize this activity
in the form of theoretical operations

> (in fact, *θεωρία* at one point
> meant "a looking at, a beholding"
> and the verb belonging to thought, *νοεῖν*,
> "to perceive with the mind")

When we already know
there are other things going on
in our heads

Preconceptual thought
Unnerving concept

But anyway
that bold process
when thought is moving at enormous speed
light-years faster than the articulation of concepts
and sentences
in the mass of letters and words
traced by the reader's eyes

Yeats:

"The purpose of rhythm is to prolong the moment of
contemplation, the moment
when we are both asleep and awake, by
hushing us with an alluring sense of monotony,
while it holds us waking by variety,
to keep us in that state of trance,
in which the mind,
liberated from the pressure of the will,
is unfolded in symbols."

RZA:

"Cause rhyme thoughts travel at a tremendous speed
Clouds of smoke, natural blends of weed"

Some things
do not travel
in the form of causal exposition
some things take flight

Dust
vampire bats at night

Surely we can think of rhythm and rhyme
in other registers

The mind unfolded in other fields

It is true that we lack control
of our social metabolism with nature

Stoffwechsel

But it does not follow
that we are better off
without the means to run other
circulatory systems
interconnected and autonomous
(like a fetus in the womb)

blood does not only flow, red
and thick
it happens to carry one or two things

I will give you an illustration
it is the angel of menstruation

In 1973 Cecilia Vicuña painted
the angel, naked
flying above the grass
and a snake of sand

The figure bled
playing with a string
her eyes red
I use my blood for looking

3

Landscape
sand dunes, hills
grey and beige
slopes lead up and down to the beach

Every Sunday a family
has the same picnic
wind a lot
rain unless it's too much
snow, sometimes
sky a lot
sun a lot

but what is a family

α

Tears are my sisters.
Humankind is glass

β

These is bloody shoes

It is more like a field of sand
than a pit.
A plateau
sheltered by humps
hairy with grass and reed
one of them
touches the sky
above the rest
majestic, towering
like the barricade at Place de la Concorde
the largest in Paris
two stories high
thousands of cobblestones

γ Gaillard

Of all the arts
the art of the shoe
is the most difficult, the most useful
and the least understood

Third objection:

This impeachment of art
is seriously flawed
in its guiding assumption
that art should awaken us,
make us conscious
or that
art itself
must produce, and embody
social change

There are, and have been, such works of art.
In May 1871, when the Paris Commune
prepared to defend itself
against the onslaught of the French army
there was one of particular symbolic importance

A shoemaker has himself photographed
in front of the barricade he has erected in the street
As has been suggested,
he indeed “signs” his barricade

In the general revolutionary fervor
La Fédération des artistes de Paris
on the evening of April 14
admitted the right to sign works
also to craftsmen and artisans, collapsing the most
unpenetrable of walls encircling
artistic production and authorship.

The result was indeed
an art *unseparated* from *social reality*.

The man in the photograph
is Napoléon Gaillard
worker, artist-shoemaker, and
subsequent author of a treatise on the foot

Posing with his hand on his hip,
in front of a work so remarkable
for its utility in the struggle for socialism

However, the coalition
of the beautiful and the practical
was as short-lived as the Commune itself.

Our perfect artwork
belongs
like a fish in water
to a seven-week period in the 19th century,
in a single city
under siege.

Already
an art
sealed off
from everything else?

In fact, the value critic of the glass prison
did suggest a way out

"Only an art of negative reflection
making us conscious of the insufferability of the economized
world can overcome itself and return to life."

Apart from the peculiarity
of providing a non-structural solution
to the structural problem he himself had sketched out

        offering, in the last few lines,
        an echo of everything
        the text up to this point had ridiculed and torn apart

it is a good example of the widespread notion
that art should
wake us from our slumber
and make us conscious

So, if it is not one, it is the other:
If art cannot embody the physical bastions of socialism
it must return to life
by making us conscious
of the dreadfulness of capitalism

There are some problems
with this idea.

First, it is predictable.

Second, such revelations
are not necessarily helpful
(blending all too well with melancholia and paralysis)

Third, it assumes passivity
and ignorance on the part of the spectator
that must be led towards consciousness
and emancipation

Again, the heroics of the avant-garde:
the military formation
marching before the rest of the army
the party before the rest of the working class
the central committee before the rest of the party

Now what if the avant-garde
is not taken as yardstick
but monumental misrepresentation
of an actual relation

A highly influential
but nonetheless
failed political and aesthetic model
of modernism

Failed: not in terms of what the avant-garde
achieved as artists, but as avant-garde.

We would then have an art
extended to its audience
on completely different terms

The barricade that people called Château Gaillard due to its
size and its creator's attempt at luxury

is beautiful
not because
it fulfills art's revolutionary purpose
by embodying
the actual working existence
of a certain *communisme*

all artworks can't be barricades, can they now

It is beautiful
because it fulfills its own purpose
which happens to coincide
with the luxurious embodiment above

And which in general may be defined as
fabrication under the attempt
to establish and adhere to its own rules

Literary scholar Kristin Ross,
in her account of the Commune
invokes John Ruskin
and the Victorian art critic's definition:

Art is what occurs when there is joy in labor.

Such a cheerful disposition
might not reflect all aspects of an artistic process
but it says something about Château Gaillard:
by making it a work of art, Gaillard did not only state
something about the categories of beauty, but
about categories of labor.

The defense structure of the Commune becomes a work of art
because of the free and joyful labor in its construction
A labor that was one of the objectives
of the Commune itself.

This right to one's own labor
is what Parisians, after sixty days of self-government,
were ready to die for, on top of its very monuments
It was what, to those on the side of order and private property,
constituted such a crime, that simply reconquering the city
militarily was not enough:
The summary executions,
going from house to house, lasted for a week

La semaine sanglante

Only after the massacres, work.

The brutality
of the division of labor

Casts long shadows
over every partition

and yet it seems unwise
to surrender a remaining domain
– sand castles, sand writing –
for a labor that owns itself

Like rituals of crypto-believers
Like the memory of popular organization
that passes through generations with the work of unions,
occupations, and free associations
something else entirely passes through this windy field

Incorporating also
The activity of looking
The joy of beholding
That which whispers a thousand different things
Inherent in Gaillard's barricade
and his other creation,
the molded *gutta-percha* shoes

These shoes
looked less like shoes than the box they come in

Sculptural elements
made for the foot not as it is, but as it should be

Gaillard had fled to Zürich,
and opened a tavern for other exiled Communards
a rare survivor,
he continued to make useful objects.

While shoes are widely recognized
for not providing the actual walking
this is a rare insight in matters of art
Despite the fundamental uncertainty of its use value
walking is expected to commence on its own

Opposed to such pedestrian fantasies
of being marched towards life
it seems that a particular possibility
lies in the labor
that determines the utility of every artwork
a labor that, in the final instance, lies with the spectator.
Of course, the artist can give some clues

The enormous amount of cobblestones making up the base
of Gaillard's barricade
far from original use and exchange values
has the stone cutter's work
vibrate in the singing of stone

In any case
Is it really so strange
if art does not
break the glass for good
to merge with every other human activity
when these appear as relations between things

Relieved of its duties
universal emancipation
and coalescence with life,
Art may remain within its field
within a general set
of known and unknown rules

It may attempt to break out
by writing its own law
In the event of such autonomy
the existing framework will simply reconfigure
and enclose the artwork anew.

Maybe art then consists
in this attempted escape?
Escape artists, *Entfesselungskunst*

escapology
and eschatology

a kind of wrestling
with the unknown

with that
which is carried by the storm

Dust
matter

muddy water

The substantial question
can only ever be answered
in form

Form looks
in other ways

Thought images
with a hyphen

From one end appears
the accountant of days
in her father's retailored suit
the short-haired author of Germany's cultural history

of daily gestures
an accumulation
beyond the intelligible

What happens here
thought images

Denkbilder

all behind glass

δ Darboven

There is nothing to describe
writing writing
I don't describe
I write.

From the other end
the measurer of particles
and another kind of time

The folding of the transparent wall
into slender cylinders
that need not be broken
but grow more fragile, cloud,
and deteriorate over the years

ε Hesse

to extend my art perhaps into
something that doesn't exist yet

In between
inzwischen
left to us,
not so much
the task of making sense,
but a sensible
making of thought

—

I came upon
these judges of art

And their
Exhibition object
in a sterilized and dead sphere
behind glass

just around the time
of the London primate escape

This creature short of words, it seems,
had something to say
on the issue of autonomy
and the limits of the glass cage

It went out

through
the glass
slipped past

The fact
that it is the same out there
does add a twist

it is only an instant
but some of the most important
parts of life
happen in instants

It made me recall
a passage by Adorno
which appears right after he has declared
his faith in the enigmatic nature of art:

“In its clownishness, art consolingly recollects
prehistory in the primordial world of animals.
Apes in the zoo
together perform
what resembles clown routines.

In the similarity of clowns to animals
the likeness of humans to apes flashes up;

Do you really know what to do,
to tell them apart?

the constellation animal/fool/clown
is a fundamental layer of art.”

The political utility of art
does not consist
in the infinite sadness of a zoo

But in the joyful moment
of passing through

glass
dust, grey matter

it all passes through
the wrestler's sinew

Brutes
Particles
Menschen
swerve in
ascension

I sit on the balcony
waxing strong
as morning touches horizon

Notes

Page 6 “London Zoo gorilla escaped ‘through open cage door,’” *The Telegraph*, 14 October 2016
“Gorilla recaptured after escape at London zoo,” *The Guardian*, 16 October 2016.

Pages 8-10 Robert Kurz, “De sköna konsternas vålnad – Varför samhället inte längre kan reflektera sig själv estetiskt i moderniteten,” *Kris och Kritik*, no. 5/6, August 2015. (Original German version: “Das Phantom der Schönen Künste – Warum sich die Gesellschaft in der Moderne nicht mehr ästhetisch reflektieren kann,” 2001, accessed August 01, 2021, https://www.exit-online.org/textanz1. php?tabelle=schwerpunkte&index=11&posnr= 103&backtext1=text1.php).

Page 11 Anselm Jappe, “Finns det en konst efter konstens slut?,” *Kris och Kritik*, no. 5/6, August 2015. (Original French version: “Est-ce qu’il y a un art après la fin de l’art?,” 2009, published May 11, 2009, http://www.palim-psao.fr/article-31273685.html).

Page 12 For the dialectics of aesthetic use value and reification in relation to the so-called Neo-avant-garde, see Benjamin Buchloh, *Neo-Avantgarde and Culture Industry: Essays on European and American Art from 1955 to 1975*, Cambridge, MA: MIT Press, 2001. See also Lucy Lippard, *Five Years: The Dematerialization of the Art Object from 1966 to 1972*, New York: Praeger, 1973.
For the art market and commodification, see Julian Stallabrass, *Art Incorporated*, Oxford: Oxford UP, 2004.

Page 13 — Sarah Liz Degerhammar & Nina Jeppson, "Konsten att skapa overklighet," Steven Cuzner, "Konsten som inte finns," *Brand*, no. 3, 2016.

Page 20 — Khaled Hourani, *The Zebra Copy Card*, 2009. Postcard, edition of 10,000.

Page 21 — Aesop, "The Ass Carrying Salt," *The Complete Fables*, trans. Olivia Temple, London: Penguin, 1998. See also "The Merchant, The Donkey, and the Salt," *Aesop's Fables*, trans. Laura Gibbs, Oxford: Oxford UP, 2002.

Page 27 — Dave Beech, *Art and Value: Art's Economic Exceptionalism in Classical, Neoclassical and Marxist Thought*, Chicago: Haymarket, 2016, 26, 254, 266.

Page 39 — Transcriptions from the Greek: *theoria*, *noein*.

Pages 41, 44 — Concerning rhythm, see W. B. Yeats, "The Symbolism of Poetry," *The Dome*, April 1900. See also George Thomson, *Marxism and Poetry*, London: Lawrence and Wishart, 1987.

Page 47 — Cecilia Vicuña, *Angel de la Menstruación*, 1973. Oil on canvas, 48.2 x 57.1 cm.

Page 51 — Anne Carson, *Men in the Off Hours*, New York: Vintage Books, 2000.

Page 51 — Cardi B, "Bodak Yellow," *Invasion of Privacy*, Atlantic, 2017.

Page 53 — Napoléon Gaillard, as quoted in Kristin Ross, *Communal Luxury*, London/New York: Verso, 2015, 50-59.

Page 55 Ross, *Communal Luxury*, 50-59.

Page 58 Kurz, "De sköna konsternas vålnad," 15.

Page 61 Eric Hazan, *La barricade: Histoire d'un objet révolutionnaire*, Paris: Autrement, 2013.

Page 62 Ross, *Communal Luxury*, 50-59; I am highly indebted to this book.

Page 64 The description of Gaillard's shoes provided by Ross is taken from Lucien Descaves's 1913 historical novel about Communard exiles, *Philémon, vieux de la vieille*. This fictional representation differs from Gaillard's own early account (including sketches). See Napoléon Gaillard, *Mémoire descriptif de la chaussure française en gutta-percha*, Paris: Henri Plon, 1857.

Page 64-67 In the argument of these pages, "art" in the indefinite form does in no way refer to the general category of "all art," in order to define its common capabilities. We have already seen this abstraction dissolve once, when it was demonstrated that it is no necessary consequence of, nor congruent with, the artistic mode of production, since this does not consist of abstract labor (p. 27). And while the criticism of those who denounce art *tout court* applies to most of contemporary art – the irrelevance, the inability to critically grasp the social divisions and historical-material conditions at its base – the same critics tend to overlook, by determination or ignorance, the few and rare works of real force, beauty, or reflection. In these pages, "art" refers precisely to such works. This is not to confuse the standards, but simply due to a lack of interest in the former, and a belief in the importance of a discussion of the latter.

Page 68 Hanne Darboven, *Kulturgeschichte 1880-1983 (Cultural History 1880-1983)*, 1980-1983. Mixed media, dimensions variable.

Page 69 Darboven in letter to Sol LeWitt, in *Hanne Darboven: Abstract Correspondence*, New York: Castelli, 2013, 12.

Page 70 Eva Hesse, *Repetition Nineteen III*, 1968. Fiberglass and polyester resin, nineteen units.

Page 71 Hesse in conversation with Cindy Nemser, "Interview with Eva Hesse," *Artforum*, May 1970.

Page 80 Theodor W. Adorno, *Aesthetic Theory*, New York: Continuum Impacts, 2004, 159.

Page 81 Rainer Maria Rilke, "The Man Watching" from *Selected Poems of Rainer Maria Rilke, A Translation from the German and Commentary by Robert Bly*, New York: Harper and Row, 1981, 105.

Page 83 Emily Dickinson, "A Little East of Jordan," from *The Poems of Emily Dickinson: Variorum Edition, 3 volumes*, ed. Ralph W. Franklin, Cambridge, MA, London: The Belknap Press of Harvard UP, 1998, 72.